T0365844

Sweet & Sassy Sistas

Table of Contents

Copyright © 2016 by Linda Felton. 753067

ISBN: Softcover   978-1-5245-5950-2
         EBook   978-1-5245-5949-6

All rights reserved. No part of this book may be
reproduced or transmitted in any form or by
any means, electronic or mechanical, including
photocopying, recording, or by any information
storage and retrieval system, without permission in
writing from the copyright owner.

Print information available on the last page

Rev. date: 12/14/2016

To order additional copies of this book, contact:
Xlibris
1-888-795-4274
www.Xlibris.com
Orders@Xlibris.com

THEO'S
Sweet & Sassy Cuisine

A Keepsake Collection of Recipes & Reflections

Written by Linda Felton

Foreword

Every community has its legends. Here in the Southern Tier of New York, one of our treasured legends centers on Theo and Barbara Felton, their family, their faith and their restaurant. Theo (short for Theodore Roosevelt) and Barbara grew up in the south and learned classic southern cooking from family and friends. Each brought their own family recipes with them when they settled on the north side of the Village of Endicott. First it was folks at church suppers and the like that marveled at Theo's barbecue and Barbara's sweet potato pie. Then others became aware of the broad range of southern style dishes that brought rave reviews. So it was a natural progression for Theo and Barbara to go to the next step and along with their kids, operated Theo's Southern Style Cuisine where you could literally taste the south in your mouth… a play on the slogan that appeared on their menu.

Like many communities, our local newspaper conducts a "Reader's Choice Awards" survey and year after year, Theo's would come out on top in at least a couple of categories. Wings for sure and more often than not barbecue. Theo created his own sauces, later bottled and still available in retail shops. The mouth-watering array of menu choices, all with a soulful touch, boggled the mind. Cornbread made fresh multiple times a day. Collard greens fixed like they do in Georgia. Catfish, ribs, pulled pork and wings. Big juicy wings slathered with Theo's special sauce. And if you were disciplined enough to save room for dessert, you would have exhibited really good judgement because you could top off your meal with Barbara's classic sweet potato pie. A dessert to die for.

But there was always more than just soul food for Theo and Barbara. Their commitment to faith and family has always been unshakeable, for them another way to demonstrate "soul". This Keepsake Collection of Recipes & Reflections that their daughter, Linda, has written is a fitting tribute to a couple and their cuisine. Sweet and Sassy…indeed.

Paul VanSavage
Author, Tastes and Tales of New York's Southern Tier

Dedication

My first publication is dedicated to my family: Past, Present and Future.

God made us strong when he made us family!

Past: Our ancestors passed on valuable skills including faith, determination and endurance.

Present: Our parents passed on the same with abundant love and togetherness. It's our responsibility to preserve and pass on the strong ties that bind us together.

> Fred, Andy, Duane, Selina, Ted, Kurt and Tressa,
> Adriena & Tyrese

Future: To the love of my Life John L. Osborne, God reunited us to finish what he started but this time with the Lord directing our paths. Together we will strive to position ourselves, our children and grandchildren to become covenant heirs.

> Linda L. Felton

Rooted and Grounded in Love

Unconditional love is the root of our foundation. Growing up with a loving close knit family has been one of the main sources that kept me grounded. Throughout this journey, I have recognized my true calling to teach others but not in the traditional school setting. My life experiences, determination and most of all my faithfulness prepared me to be a living example for others to follow their dreams and pursue their destiny.

I have found my passion and been blessed with the ability to combine all the things that I love and put them together in a keepsake to capture the family legacy for others to enjoy now and in the future.

Our Legacy & Family Tree

Felton and West
Theodore Felton
Grandparents: Robert & Viola (Lewis) Felton
Great-Grandparents: Mr. & Mrs. Tom Felton
Great-Grandparents: Mr. & Mrs. Lewis
Barbara (West) Felton
Grandparents: Milton and Bobbie Lou (Jones) West
Great-Grandparents: Henry & Mary (Holt) Jones

Theo's History

Story of Theo's Southern Style Cuisine Restaurant JC NY

Theo's Southern Style Cuisine Restaurant founded by Theodore Roosevelt Felton Sr. and Barbara Jean Felton. The business was centrally located at the historic arch in Johnson City, New York.

Founded in 1991, Theo's was a small business with a big appetite. The family restaurant cooks up home-style meals with a side of southern hospitality. Recipes have been passed down throughout the generations that date back to the ante-bellum period in South Georgia. With the migration from the Empire state of the South to the Empire State of the North in the 50's, the move from Georgia to New York opened the doors for the Felton Family and the creation of Theo's.

Awards & Honorable Mentions

- MWBE Trailblazer Award – 1999
- 1993 Broome County Black & Minority Coalition – Minority Business Achievement Award
- 1994 Delta Achievement Award
- 1998 Achievement Award
- Voted BEST in the Southern Tier by the Press & Sun Bulletin
- Readers Choice Award – Best Ribs 1993, 1995, 1998,1999
- Readers Choice Award – Best BBQ Chicken 1997, 1999, 1998
- Readers Choice Award – Best Wings 1997, 1998, 1999
- Readers Choice Award – Best BBQ 2004, 2006
- Mayor's Proclamation and Key to the City – Johnson City, New York
- Theo's Southern Style Cuisine with a New York Twist!
- Award winning for over 10 years for BBQ, Ribs, Chicken and Stylin Wings

Theo's featured in following Publications:

- Theo's featured in 1998 Edition of "Where the Local's Eat" For Best BBQ Ribs
- African American Regional Cooking Library- The Culinary Institute of America – Food images prepared by Theo's Southern Style Cuisine
- Taste & Tales of NY's Southern Tier
- Faces of the Southern Tier 2006
- What's Cooking at Olums – Local TV Show

Theo's Community Activities & Events :

- McGregory BBQ At the Winery in NYS Finger Lake
- Oh Taste & See Celebration – Expanded Binghamton's First Friday activities to Johnson City by featuring the diverse cuisine of the south combined with displays of local artists: Kathye Edwina Arrington (African American) and Elbert White (Native American)
- Tioga County Council of the Arts Festival – Hickory Smoked Blues
- Corning NY Arts Festival – Corning Museum of Glass

Upstate NY Facts

Upstate NY —Upstate New York is the portion of the State of New York lying north of New York City. The region includes most of the state of New York, excluding New York City. Upstate provides a variety of natural resources including fruit production, honey, wine and dairy products.

Broome County is located in New York's Southern Tier, southeast of the Finger Lakes and just north of Pennsylvania. Broome County is known as the "Carousel Capital of the World" Only 19 historical carousels still exist and 6 are located in Broome County parks.

The region has been called the "Triple Cities" which is made up of Binghamton, Johnson City and Endicott. All three have significant roles which are provided throughout the history.

Village of Johnson City, NY- Home of the Square Deal- Site of Theo's Restaurant

Village of Endicott – Home of the Square Deal - Endicott is best known as the "Birthplace of IBM". Linda began her 25 year career at IBM.

Our neighborhood on the North side of Endicott is where we resided since I was 2 years old (56 years ago). Our parents still live in the same house that we grew up in and raised a family of 8 children.

One of the beautiful carousels is in my neighbor and as children growing up; we never had to pay to ride it. Now I have the wonderful pleasure of taking our grandchildren, nieces and nephews to the same park where they can also enjoy the carousel. They have been restored, preserved and there will never be a fee to ride which is extremely rare considering it is a true works of art.

The Italians settled on the North Side of the village. Today the North Side is recognized as "Little Italy" and still has a large Italian population.

The reason why I included my background of having southern parents, born in Binghamton and raised in predominately Italian neighborhood will help to understand how I learned to cook diversely at a very young age. I began collecting recipes since I was seven years old from my piano teacher the late Mrs. Betty Cieri.

George F. Johnson
"If anything has been done for joy that has made you a bit happier, hand it on to somebody else just as soon as you can. That's the way to keep square with the world.' (1934)

RECOGNITION

Theodore Roosevelt Felton Sr. and Barbara Jean Felton Day
Saturday October 25, 2014

WHEREAS: Theodore Roosevelt Felton Sr .was born on October 22, 1034 and Barbara Jean Felton was born on February 22, 1939, and migrated from South GA to Upstate NY; and

WHEREAS: Theodore and Barbara recently celebrated 60 years of marriage on August 4, 2014; and

WHEREAS: Theodore celebrated his 80th birthday on October 22, 2014 and within 8 decades along with Barbara, raised 8 children which blessed them with 13 Grandchildren and 4 Great-Grandchildren; and

WHEREAS: Theodore and Barbara moved to the North Side of Endicott in 1956 and have been long time outstanding residents in the community; and

WHEREAS: Theodore and Barbara encouraged extended family members to move to the Triple Cities for employment opportunities to make a better life for their families; and

WHEREAS: Theodore and Barbara earned the respect of others by being real life approachable role models, and willingly shared their wisdom by demonstrating commitment to their family, marriage, church community and business; and

WHEREAS: Theodore and Barbara and the entire Felton family added diversity and southern cuisine to our community and opened Theo's Southern Style Cuisine Restaurant; and

WHEREAS: Theodore and Barbara used their gifts to serve and provide down home cooking for over 20 years and were recognized by the Press and Sun Bulletin Readers Choice Awards for having the best Wings, BBQ and Chicken for over 10 years; and

NOW, THEREFORE I, John R. Bertoni, by virtue of the authority vested in me as Mayor of the Village of Endicott do hereby deem it an honor and pleasure to proclaim this day, Saturday, October 25th, 2014 as Theodore and Barbara Felton Day for their service and love of the Village of Endicott and Broome County. We extend to them our deep appreciation for their dedication and contributions to our community and wish them many years of health and happiness; and now please join me and the Felton family in proclaiming this: **Theodore and Barbara Felton Day**

Mayor John R. Bertoni

Theo's Classics

Theo's Sweet Potato Fries

3 – 4 medium Sweet Potatoes
Vegetable Oil
Sugar/Cinnamon Mixture
Cut potatoes into ½ inch strips with peels on
Soak for 15 minutes in mixture of sugar/water
(½ cup water with 2 tbsp of sugar)

....

Drain excess water. Coat potatoes with oil and place on baking sheet (sprayed with Pam). Bake about 15 minutes on each side. Remove from pan and sprinkle with cinnamon-sugar mixture.

Potatoes can also be deep fried or pan fried for 5 minutes or until crispy.

....

Grammy's Yammies

6-8 medium Sweet Potatoes
1 cup butter
1 cup sugar
1 tablespoon cinnamon
1 teaspoon nutmeg
1 teaspoon vanilla extract

....

Peel and slice potatoes lengthwise and place in large Dutch oven. Add butter, sugar, spices and vanilla. Cover and cook on low heat until potatoes are tender. No additional liquid is needed. The potatoes will make their own juices.

....

Theo's Coleslaw

1 head of cabbage
2- 3 carrots (peeled)
Real mayonnaise
¼ cup Vinegar
Sugar to taste

Use grate blade on food processor and grate cabbage including dark leaves. Place in separate bowl and grate carrots in processor. Mix with fork until cabbage and carrots are blended well. In small bowl mix mayonnaise, sugar and vinegar until smooth. Pour over cabbage and refrigerator until ready to serve. Excellent with fried fish or BBQ.

Theo's BBQ Pork Sandwich

Lean Pork Tenderloin or Pork Butt
Theo's all purpose seasoning (Or favorite BBQ seasoning)
Theo's BBQ Sauce or Theo's Hot & Spicy Sauce

Wash and pat meat dry. Add seasoning and rub into meat. Slow roast meat on hot grill or cook in 250* oven in covered pan for about 1 hour per pound. Internal temperature should reach 190*. Meat should be tender and shred easily with a fork. Let meat rest for at least one hour before pulling or chopping. Place in sauce pan and add sauce or serve with sauce on the side. Serve on fresh bun with side of Theo's homemade coleslaw.

Theo's was one of the first area restaurants to introduce BBQ Pork Sandwiches with Coleslaw and now you can find in many of the southern tier establishments. The coleslaw was always homemade using local fresh ingredients.

Theo's BBQ Beef

15- 20 lb top round beef
Kosher Salt
Garlic Pepper
Theo's all purpose Seasoning

....

Rinse meat and pat dry then season with above or your favorite beef seasonings. Place in roaster pan, cover with foil and cook at 250* in oven or slow cook in smoker for appropriate 4 hours or until done. Once meat is done and cooled, thin slice or chop and serve with Theo's Southern Style BBQ sauce or Theo's Hot & Spicy BBQ for a little kick.

....

Theo's BBQ beef was featured at BBQ at the Winery a yearly event held at McGregory's Winery one of the oldest wineries in the Finger Lake Region in Upstate New York.

This is dedicated to all of those who have learned their hardest and sweetest lessons through the things that they have lost. May you not only find wisdom on the path to restoration, but also discover the most amazing truth of all - success in life is not found in whom you become or the things you acquire. At the end of the day, whom others become because of your presence will be remembered far longer. Here's to the joy and peace that knowledge brings to your life."

Michelle McKinney Hammond

Theo's Apple Crumb Pie

3 -4 firm apples (we use Cortland Apples)
Peel, core and slice
½ cup butter
½ cup sugar
2 teaspoon cinnamon
Crumb topping
1 cup flour
½ cup sugar
¼ cup brown sugar
1 ½ teaspoon cinnamon
1 stick butter

8- 9 inch Pie Shell-homemade or prepared

Spray apples with lemon juice to prevent browning. Mix sugar and butter. Add apples Place in prepared pie shell. Mix all crumb topping dry items and cut butter into with fork.

Top with crumb mixture and bake until browned at 350 degrees 45 — 60 minutes.

Everything's Just Sweet & Sassy

Theo's Sweet & Sassy is one of 3 signature sauces used at the Legendary Theo's Southern Style Restaurant. A versatile addition to everything from Meatballs, Crab Cakes, Egg Rolls and even popcorn!

Tressa, Linda & Selina

Sweet & Sassy Chicken Wings

3 lbs fresh chicken wings
Theo's All Purpose Seasoning
Cooking Oil

....

Heat oil in deep fryer to 375* wash and lightly season wings. Coat with flour and slowly drop into hot oil. Fry until crispy approximately 10 minutes (depending on wing size). While wings are frying, pour Sweet & Sassy sauce in a medium bowl with lid. When wings are done, drain then add to sauce in bowl. Cover tightly and shake to completely coat wings. Use same recipe for all wings and coat with Theo's Hot & Spicy or Theo's BBQ Sauce. Serve with celery sticks and dressing of choice.

....

Sweet & Sassy Tempura Shrimp

1 lb shrimp
⅔ cup all purpose flour
½ teaspoon salt
Theo's All purpose seasoning
½ teaspoon baking soda
1 tablespoon vinegar
⅔ cup water
Theo's Sweet & Sassy Sauce
cooking oil

....

Heat oil in deep fat fryer to 375* devein and clean shrimp. Drain and lightly season shrimp. Mix flour and salt in medium bowl. Dissolve the baking soda in vinegar and add to water. Mix liquid into flour and stir until smooth. Add seasoned shrimp to batter and coat evenly. Carefully drop one at a time into hot oil and fry for 3-4 minutes or until golden brown. Drain on paper towel then remove to clean platter. Drizzle Sweet & Sassy over shrimp and serve hot. Can also coat shrimp completely then sprinkle Sesame Seeds to create **Sweet & Sassy Sesame Shrimp.**

....

Reflection: Tempura Shrimp is the most requested item that I have to make for my brothers and sisters every trip home. Salt potatoes, Theo's wings, Nirchi's pizza and Spiedies our weekend favorites!

Sweet & Sassy Salmon

1 pound salmon fillets
¼ teaspoon ground ginger
1 teaspoon Old Bay Seasoning
Theo's Sweet & Sassy Sauce

....

Preheat skillet lightly coated with olive oil and butter. Season salmon and place top down in hot oil. Pan sear for 2-3 minutes then turn to skin-side down. Glaze Salmon with Sweet & Sassy Sauce and continue baking for 10 minutes or until it flakes easily with fork.

....

Sweet & Sassy Pork Kabobs

2 lbs pork tenderloin (cubed)
Pineapple Juice
Fresh Ginger (chopped)
Bell Peppers (Red & Green)
Can of Pineapple Chunks

....

Marinate pork cubes in pineapple juice and fresh ginger. Soak wooded skewers in water. String skewers alternating with pork, red peppers, green peppers, pineapple cubes. Place on prepared grill and rotate to cook evenly. Brush with Sweet & Sassy sauce after grilling and before serving.

....

Sweet & Sassy Stir Fry

1 bunch Broccoli florets
1 lb Snow Peas
Bell Peppers (green, yellow, red, orange)
1 lb Carrots (julienned)
1 can Water Chestnut
1 lb - Baby Portobello mushrooms
Green Onions
Fresh garlic

Cut all vegetables into bite size portions. Heat oil in large wok over medium heat, cook garlic till lightly brown then and add peppers and onions. Add remaining ingredients and cook for few minutes until slightly tender. Add Sweet & Sassy sauce and simmer 2 more minutes. I use fresh vegetables when available but the frozen stir fry vegetables work well. Prepare same as above with fresh garlic, then after cooking add Sweet & Sassy sauce in place of Soy or Duck sauce. (Less sodium)

All about the Honey

Mom always insists we use only the best quality ingredients in every item made at Theo's and at home.

Honey is the main ingredient in Theo's Sweet & Sassy sauce but not just any honey! While searching for a honey supplier, we discovered that Upstate New York offers all kinds of information on honey bees, bee-keepers and bee pollination. Over the years we tried many suppliers and have been able to create a consistent product every time. What set's our current supplier apart from the rest is the master beekeeper's years of experience added to his will and desire to keep learning from the bees.

The method used to extract and bottle the honey is to limit the processing to keep the high quality standards customers need to make a high quality product. Recognizing where their gift comes from and giving God the Glory is proudly displayed on their website and that is why I am proud to include Kutik's Honey in my book and in our sauces. "The result is a full-bodied taste, preserving all the God-Given and healthful properties of nature's oldest sweetener." Reference – website and National Honey Board

I am fascinated with the entire process and can write a whole chapter on honey but one important Honey tip: Look for the ***True Source Certified*** logo.

Healthy Cuisine

In honor of the late Herman C. Shelton, this section is dedicated to all the people that put their family, friends and neighborhood children first. Herman devoted most of his life to putting the needs of others before his own.

God was the head of his Herman's life and he was blessed with many spiritual gifts. His gift to serve was put to great use and not only did he serve in the US Army, he also was very active in church and devoted quality time with the neighborhood children as a football coach, basketball referee and the best supporter of his children and all their friends throughout grade school and beyond.

After Herman suffered with a stroke and had heart value replacement, I had to put my business on hold and delayed publishing this book to become a fulltime caregiver. During his illness he helped me to discover my true passion of making a difference in others lives by sharing my gifts using food as the common unifier.

I began volunteering with the American Heart Association and American Stroke Association to learn more about Herman's condition and became an advocate and eventually began doing food demonstrations for both organizations. I met people from all walks of life and was surprise to have met so many young people dealing with heart and stroke disease.

My focus was to show others how to modifying foods and make them more heart healthy. The challenge was trying to convince adults to change their eating habits so I concentrated on the children first. "Children learn what they live" yet they are more open to trying new things especially when it is presented in a manner to keep their attention. By making good nutrition choices along with positive influences, children can share their experiences with the entire family. Together we can all work towards simple lifestyle changes which are the key to living a long and healthier life.

Best lesson learned is to follow the tried and tested method that worked back in the day and still can work today if we pass on the blessings we received from our mothers and grandmothers.

Linda's passion expanded throughout North TX and the Dallas area. The opportunity to provide healthy cuisine to a variety of organizations has been very rewarding.

Kwanza Fest
Go Red Dallas
MLK Fest
Power to End Stroke
Goodnews UT Southwestern Division of community medicine
Ministry at FBC – Acteens – young girls cooking classes
Holiday Cookie baking – girls & boys – yearly tradition

Learning to cooking using different ingredients, fresh herbs and oils opened up a whole new world of foods that are good for you. For example I loved snap peas but never knew they were a Legume!

Legumes-Any plant with Seed Pods that split into half, such as snap peas

5 Things to reduce or eliminate from diet:

1)   **Salt**
2)   **Sugar**
3)   **Starch**
4)   **Caffeine**
5)   **Unsaturated Fats**

Drink half your body weight in water daily and Know your key numbers:

Weight, Blood pressure, Blood Sugar, Cholesterol

I Encourage readers to take the journey with me by committing to making gradual lifestyle changes that can improve overall well being and increase longevity! Make food choices for a future that allows the ability to inspire and not be restricted or limited by illness. Preventative when possible is the key!

Easy Asian Chicken Lettuce Wraps

1 tablespoon sesame oil
¼ cup Hoisin sauce*
(*I use Sweet & Sassy sauce)
1 tablespoon low-sodium soy sauce
½ teaspoon ground ginger
2 cups shredded or chopped cooked chicken

⅓ cup chopped water chestnuts
⅓ cups sliced pea pods
¼ cups shredded carrots
¼ cup green onions
Lettuce leaves

....

Combine sesame oil, hoisin sauce, soy sauce and ginger in small bowl. Place the chicken, water chestnuts, pea pods, carrots and onions in large bowl and pour the sesame oil mixture over chicken. Toss gently to coat. Place spoonful of the chicken on a piece of lettuce, roll up and tuck edges under.

....

Field Greens Salad with Strawberries

12 cups of field greens
2 fresh apples sliced thing (your choice)
1 cups fresh strawberries sliced
¼ cup toasted almonds

Strawberry Vinaigrette

Double this recipe to use half to marinate the chicken and the other half for salad dressing.

⅓ cups strawberry preserves
⅓ cup balsamic vinegar
⅓ cup raspberry wine vinegar
1 teaspoon of red wine vinegar
1 teaspoon olive oil
½ package dry Italian dressing

Grilled Chicken

6 – 4 oz chicken breasts
1 recipe strawberry vinaigrette dressing

....

Marinate chicken in vinaigrette dressing. Place in refrigerator overnight. Grill chicken and cut into strips. Set aside and place on salads when ready to serve.

....

Regional Favorites

Fresh Herb Dressing

1 ½ cp loosely packed parsley
½ cups loosely packed basil
¼ cup loosely packed oregano
¼ cup any favorite herb of choice
¼ cup loosely packed chives
2 cloves garlic
2 cups olive oil
Salt and pepper to taste

....

Wash and dry all herbs and chop finely. (I use food processor)

Crush garlic cloves and chop finely. Add olive oil, mix in herbs and add salt and pepper to taste Use as a dressing, meat marinade or to dip bread into.

....

Down Home Cabbage

1 medium 2 lb cabbage, cut up
2 teaspoon salt
1 medium onion, chopped
1 medium pepper, chopped
2 tablespoon flour
2 tablespoon sugar
¼ cup cider vinegar
⅛ teaspoon pepper
6 slices of turkey bacon

In large pot add 1 inch water to boiling. Add cabbage and salt. Return to boil; cover and cook 5 minutes. Drain well reserving 1 ¼ cups cooking liquid. Keep cabbage warm cook bacon until crisp then remove and add onion and bell pepper. Sauté until tender then sprinkle in flour and sugar. Stir until smooth. Stir in reserved cooking liquid, vinegar and pepper. Cook over medium heat stirring constantly until thickened. Add bacon and cabbage stir gently until coated.

Upstate City Chicken

1 lb cubed meat (choice of veal, pork or chicken)
Salt, pepper, garlic and parsley
Italian Bread Crumbs

....

Season meat then place on wooden skewers. Shake in bag with flour to coat evenly. Dip skewers in egg mixture (2 eggs and 2 tablespoon milk) beaten.

Roll in bread crumbs and lightly brown on both sides in hot oil then place in baking dish, cover and bake at 300* for 35 – 55 minutes or until done. Chicken can be used in place of veal or pork. Season chicken and flour then continue with same steps, dip skewers in egg mixture and roll in breadcrumbs and brown on both sides before placing in oven.

....

Homemade Chow-Chow GA

4 cups of white onions
4 cups of green cabbage
4 cups of green tomatoes
12 green bell peppers
6 red peppers
½ cup kosher salt
6 cups sugar
1 teaspoon celery seeds
2 tablespoon mustard seeds
1 ½ teaspoon turmeric
4 cups cider vinegar
2 cups water

Wash all vegetables, drain well then grind using a course blade in food processor. Sprinkle ½ of salt over the grounded vegetables. Cover and let stand overnight at room temperature. Rinse and drain. Combine remaining ingredients, sugar, celery seeds, mustard seeds, turmeric, vinegar and water.

Pour into vegetable mixture. Heat to a boil then simmer for only 3 minutes. Pour into hot sterilized jars and seal to makes 8 pints. Serve with greens, vegetable or as a relish.

Homemade Brunswick Stew

6 lbs pork
6 pounds chicken
3 lbs tomatoes
4 large onions (chopped)
2 cups whole kernel corn
3 large potatoes (diced)
3 cups tomato catsup
2 teaspoon black pepper
3 teaspoon red pepper
3 teaspoon salt
½ cup vinegar
Water for desired consistency

Check meats on hand in freezer before buying more. Can use boston butts, ham, turkey and chicken. English peas, lima beans can also be used. Cook chicken separate then debone and add to rest of meat that has been seasoned and simmered for at least 1 ½ hours. Add remaining vegetables and simmer 30 more minutes adding water or chicken broth for desired consistency. Season to taste and serve with cornbread. Makes 15 quarts and freezes well.

John's favorite Cornbread

1 ½ stick of butter (melted)
1 cup of corn meal
¾ cup all purpose flour
2 teaspoons sugar
1 ½ teaspoon baking powder
½ teaspoon baking soda
¼ teaspoon salt
1 ½ cup buttermilk
2 eggs light beaten

Preheat the oven to 425 degrees

Lightly grease an 8 inch glass baking dish In large bowl mix together: cornmeal, flour, sugar, baking powder,baking soda and salt In a separate bowl mix together: eggs, buttermilk and butter. Pour the buttermilk mixture into the cornmeal and fold together until there are no dry spots. Mix together well. Pour into the prepared dish. Bake until the top is golden brown. Insert a toothpick in the middle of cornbread to see if it is done. Cook for 20 to 25 minutes. Cool for 10 minutes before serving.

Carolina Chew Cakes

½ cup margarine, softened
1-16 oz package light brown sugar
3 eggs
2 cups self rising flour
1 Teaspoon vanilla
1 Cup chopped pecans

....

Cream margarine and sugar until light and fluffy. Add Eggs and beat well. Beat in flour, vanilla then add nuts. Spoon batter into a well grease and lightly floured 13x9x2 inch pan. Bake at 300 degrees for 45 minutes. Cool and cut into squares. 2 ½ Dozen

....

Old Fashion Tea Cakes

2 cups sugar
3 cups all purpose flour
4 eggs
1 cup milk
2 sticks of butter
Pinch salt
1 tablespoon baking powder
½ half teaspoon nutmeg

....

In large bowl combine sugar, butter, eggs. Blend well Sift flour with salt, baking powder and nutmeg. Add to sugar mixture add milk and mix until dough is smooth. Roll dough on lightly floured surface to ¼ inch or ½ for bigger teacakes.

Bake at 375 degrees for 8- 10 minutes

....

Texas Sheet Cake

2 cups flour
2 cups sugar
1 teaspoon baking soda
½ teaspoon salt
2 sticks butter
4 tablespoons cocoa
1 cup water
2 eggs
½ cup buttermilk
1 teaspoon vanilla

....

Preheat oven to 350* Grease and flour jellyroll pan (10x15) inches Sift the flour, sugar, baking soda and salt together in a large bowl.

Melt butter in saucepan over medium heat. Stir in Cocoa and water. Bring to a boil. Remove from heat and add dry ingredients. Mix well. Add eggs, buttermilk and vanilla and beat for 1minute. Pour into prepared pan and back for 20 minutes or until toothpick inserted comes out clean.

Remove cake from oven and spread with the chocolate icing while both cake and icing are still warm or hot.

Chocolate Icing

While cake is baking, heat 1 stick of butter, 4 tablespoon cocoa and 6 tablespoons of buttermilk in a saucepan. Stir to combine and bring to a boil. Remove from heat and combine with one box of sifted powdered sugar Beat until smooth. Stir in 1 cup of chopped pecans. Use icing before it cools. Spread evenly.

....

Mock Mint Julep - TX

2 cup cold water
1 ½ cup sugar
¾ cup lemon juice
6 mint sprigs
5 cups ice cubes
2 ½ cup ginger ale (chilled)
lemon slices and additional mint leaves

....

In large bowl combine water, sugar, lemon juice and mint. let stand for at least 45 minutes. Strain and discard mint. Place ice cubes in 2- 2 quart pitcher. Add ½ lemon mix and ginger-ale to each pitcher to make about 3 quarts. Serve in clear plastic 9 oz glasses garnished with lemon slices and mint leave.

....

*"You never really leave a place you love. Part of it you take
with you, leaving a part of yourself behind.'*

Unknown

Basic Spiedie Recipe

3 lbs lamb, beef, pork or chicken
$^2/_3$ cup red wine vinegar
$^2/_3$ cup olive oil
2 tsp oregano
2 tsp basil
1 tsp pepper
2 tsp salt
2 cloves garlic-chopped
sprigs of mint and parsley

....

Cut meat into 1 inch cubes. Blend remaining ingredients and pour over meat. Marinate overnight or for few days. String 4-6 pieces of meat on skewers and cook on hot grill for about 10 minutes or until done. Baste with remaining marinade while cookwing.

....

The beauty of this basic recipe is that it can easily be modified by adding your favorite fruits, herbs, oils and dressings. I created the Sweet & Sassy Spiedies Sandwich just by Squeezing Sweet & Sassy over meat before adding to the bread for a zesty kick!

I make spiedies wherever I travel while promoting Sweet & Sassy Sauce and have been asked the same question: **What is a Spiedie?**

"The Spiedie originated in Upstate NY and is a dish local to Greater Binghamton in the Southern Tier of New York State. A Spiedie consists of cubes of chicken, pork, lamb, veal, venison or beef. The meat cubes are marinated overnight or longer in a special marinade and then grilled on Spiedie rods."

Sweet & Sassy Sauce has also originated in Upstate NY and is very popular throughout the region. It can be served on chicken, beef, pork, fish and veggies. Sweet & Sassy Spiedie sandwich is the perfect blend of 2 regional favorites. Try experimenting with a variety of combinations to make it your own: Garlic & Honey, Lemon & Rosemary, Mango & Ginger are a few of my favorites.

Pizza Fritte (Italian Fried Dough)

3 cups of Oil
1 pound pizza dough
Powdered Sugar

....

Heat oil in large skillet (about half full), using fresh dough, break palm size pieces and stretch using gentle circular movements until the dough is a flat circle. Prick with a fork to prevent air bubbles while cooking. Once oil is hot, carefully drop dough and fry until brown then turn and brown other side. Remove promptly and drain oil on paper towel. Sprinkle lightly with powdered sugar. Serve warm.

....

Another regional favorite food that brings back mouthwatering memories is a Pizza Fritte or Italian Fried Dough. Annual festivals were held every summer on the North side of Endicott. There is a church on almost every corner. We lived diagonally cross the street from St Anthony's Church and could watch the members making the delicious treats and vividly recall watching people walk by with piles of pizza fritte's along with other delicious Italian food all weekend long.

We experienced a few additional "twists of diversity" within our local neighborhood. St. Peter & Paul's Russian Orthodox Greek Church and St Joesph's Church also specialized in selling homemade goods including Pizza Frittes, Kolachi's, Holupki's, Pieorgies and the best Nut Rolls ever! I didn't realize how diverse our neighborhood was until I moved away and came back. Now every street reminds me of the rich cultural exchange we were blessed to have as a part of our foundation and why it should be shared with everyone!

Breakfast & Brunch

Breakfast & Brunch session is dedicated to my children and grandchildren. Our family's favorite meal is the very first one each day! As the mother of two children, one of the most rewarding roles of motherhood was to be able to provide balanced, nutritious meals quickly for them every morning.

Adriena & Tyrese loved breakfast as kids and love it even more as adults. They always woke up ready to eat! The ability to feed our family is one of the most important actions that impacted the health and well being for both of them. Healthy kids grow into healthy adults.

We were raised with the simple concept and regardless of how many mouth's to feed, there are always ways to get food even it you had to grow some of it yourself. It was customary to feed large families. 8-10 kids were normal and with 2 parents, no one ever went hungry and somehow there was always food to share.

Kale & Mushroom Scrabble

Baby Portabella Mushrooms-Sliced
Fresh Kale or Spinach
2-3 eggs-beaten

....

Spray skillet with Pam and cook mushrooms until tender. Add Kale and sauté until soft. Add light salt and pepper to eggs (I use egg whites) and pour directly over the vegetables. Scrabble until eggs are done. Remove from heat and eat!

....

Tip: Anything leftovers can be made into a scrabble. Heat meats and vegetables first then add protein for quick, nutritious breakfast or brunch.

Blueberry Buckle

Cake
2 cups flour
¾ cups sugar
2 ½ teaspoon baking powder
¾ teaspoon salt
½ cup shortening
1 egg
¾ cup milk

Topping
½ cup sugar
⅓ cup flour
½ teaspoon cinnamon
¼ cup melted butter
2 cups fresh blueberries

Preheat oven to 350 degrees. Combine cake ingredients and mix well. Gently fold in blueberries. Pout into 9x9x2greased cake pan. Mix topping and sprinkle on cake. Bake 40 – 45 minutes or until toothpick inserted comes out clean.

Through we all must choose our own paths in life and the journey may sometimes seem far,
If we learn from our ancestors' struggle and strife, we will be better yet than we are.
Our grandfathers etching our history in stone and grandmothers with silken threads weaving,
Empowered us with the will to be strong and succeed if we keep on believing.

Poem by Carole Joy Gellineau

Nut Roll

6 cups flour shifted
1 teaspoon salt
½ lb butter or oleo
3 tablespoon sugar
3 eggs beaten
½ pint sour cream
2 yeast cakes
½ cup warm milk

Filling
4 cups ground walnuts
2 tablespoon honey
Sugar to taste
Warm milk to make paste
Mix nuts with sugar add honey and milk

....

Combine all ingredients except yeast and milk. Dissolve yeast in warm milk then add to rest of ingredients. Mix, knead well. Divide into 8 – 9 parts. Roll out each unto a floured board in rectangle shape. Spread with filling and roll lengthwise. Allow to rise 1 hour or until double in size. Bake at 35 – 40 minutes or until brown. Glaze with beaten egg or milk if desired.   **Amelia Pamisiani**

....

Broccoli Roll

1 pound dough
1 pound mozzarella
2 large fresh bunches of broccoli
Olive Oil, Butter and Garlic
Pepper to season

Steam the broccoli until crunchy. Lightly fry with garlic in butter and olive oil to coat pan. Roll out dough and place shredded cheese on the fried broccoli. Roll as Jelly roll. Brush top with oil, garlic and pepper. Bake at 350 degrees for 45 minutes. Let cool, slice and serve warm.

Apple Impromptu

4 cups sliced apples
¼ cups sugar
½ teaspoon cinnamon
Place in greased pie tin.

....

Seal with foil and bake for 20 minutes at 400 degrees

....

1 teaspoon butter
½ cup sugar
1 teaspoon vanilla
1 slightly beaten egg
Cream together then add:
⅔ cups flour
½ teaspoon baking powder
¼ cups chopped walnuts

....

Top apple mixture, bake for 20 minutes and serve warm with whipped cream

....

Southern Style Pimiento Cheese

8 oz bag shredded cheddar cheese
4 oz jar pimientos, drained
¼ cup mayonnaise

....

Mix together and chill before serving on sandwiches, burgers, crackers and vegetables.

....

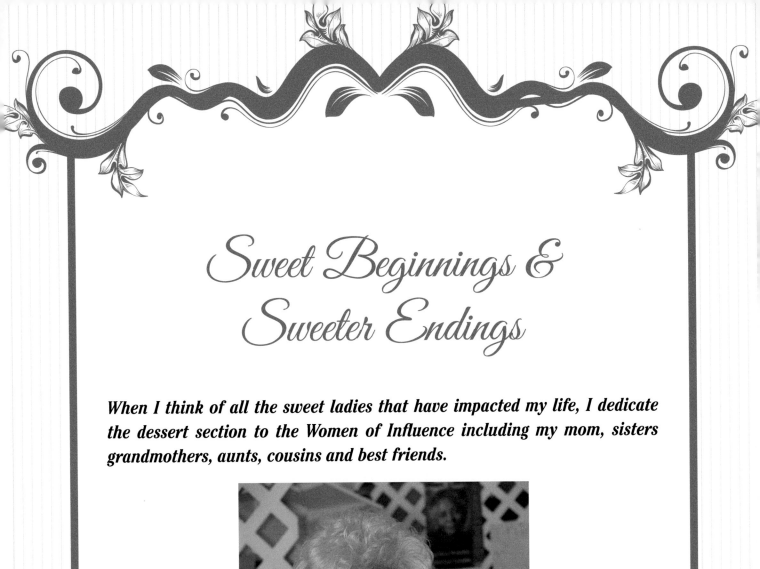

Sweet Beginnings & Sweeter Endings

When I think of all the sweet ladies that have impacted my life, I dedicate the dessert section to the Women of Influence including my mom, sisters grandmothers, aunts, cousins and best friends.

Theo's Sweet Potato Pie

Mrs. Theo Co-Founder of Theo's Southern Style Restaurant

5 Lbs Sweet Potatoes
3 Cups Sugar
2 Cups Milk
¼ Lb Butter
4 Eggs
2 Teaspoons Lemon Extract
2 Teaspoons Nutmeg

Preheat oven to 350. Rinse potatoes and boil until tender. Cool then peel. Beat with electric mixer until all lumps are gone. Add soft butter and remaining ingredients. Mix until well blended. The mix should be same consistency as pancake batter.

Place in prepared pie shell and place on baking sheet. Bake until done-about 1 hour. Cool before slicing, serve with love and enjoy!

Makes 2 - 9" pies

Chocolate Cherry Nut Cake

4 eggs

3 cups sugar

2 ½ cups plain flour

½ cup cocoa

3 teaspoon baking powder

½ cup partially melted shortening

2 teaspoons vanilla flavoring

1 ½ teaspoon almond extract

½ cup evaporated milk

½ cup chopped maraschino cherries

2 cups shopped pecans

½ cup hot water

....

Beat eggs, add sugar in one bowl. Sift flour, cocoa and baking powder together. Add to sugar mixture. Add shortening, flavoring, extract, milk, water, pecans and cherries. Mix well. Pour into a floured and greased 10 inch tube pan. Bake at 325 degrees for 1 hour and 10 minutes until done.

....

Deep Dark Chocolate Cake

1 ¾ cups flour
2 cups sugar
¾ cups cocoa
1 ½ teaspoon baking soda
1 ½ teaspoon baking powder
1 teaspoon salt

2 eggs
1 cup milk
2 teaspoon vanilla
½ cup oil
1 cup boiling water

Combine dry ingredients in mixing bowl. Add remaining ingredients except water. Beat at a medium speed for 2 minutes. Stir in water then place in floured and greased pan. Bake at 350 degrees until done.

Five Flavor Cake

2 Sticks butter or margarine
½ cup Crisco
3 cups sugar
5 eggs well beaten
3 cups all purpose flour
½ teaspoon baking powder
1 cup milk

....

1 teaspoon of each: Coconut, Rum, butter, lemon and vanilla

Cream butter, Crisco and sugar until fluffy then add eggs. Combine flour, baking powder and add to creamed mixture. Alternate with milk then stir in flavorings. Cook for 1 ½ hours in preheated over at 325 degrees.

....

New Applesauce Cake

Mix together and blend:

2 ½ cup sifted flour
1 ¾ cup sugar
¼ teaspoon baking powder
¼ teaspoon baking soda
1 teaspoon salt
¾ teaspoon cinnamon
½ teaspoon clove
½ teaspoon allspice

Add the following to the above

½ cup oil
½ cup water
½ cup walnuts
1 cup raisins (optional)

Mix for 2 minutes

1 ½ cup applesauce- Unsweetened
1 large egg

....

Add to cake mixture, blend and place in 12x9 pan (greased and floured) and bake for 45-50 minutes at 350 degrees.

....

Carrot Cake

2 cups finely grated carrots
2 cups sugar
4 eggs
1 ½ cup vegetable oil
½ cups chopped nuts

3 cups flour
2 teaspoon baking soda
2 teaspoon baking powder
2 teaspoon cinnamon
¼ teaspoon salt

....

Combine first 5 ingredients and beat well. Sift together flour, baking soda, baking powder, cinnamon and salt. Add to carrot mix. Grease and flour Bundt pan. Bake for 45 minute at 350* Remove from pan to cool then frost with Cream Cheese Frosting.

....

Cream Cheese Frosting

2 cream cheese-soften
¼ cup soften butter
1 box confectionary sugar
1 teaspoon vanilla

....

Blend until fluffy and frost carrot cake when cool.

....

Butter Rum Glaze

¼ cup plus 2 tablespoons butter
3 tablespoons rum
¾ cup sugar
3 tablespoons water
½ cup chopped walnuts (optional)

....

Combine first four ingredients in saucepan. Bring to a boil and stir constantly for 3 minutes. Remove from heat and stir in walnuts or serve without nuts.

....

Sugared Pecans

1 teaspoon water
1 egg white
Beat until frothy
Mix with 3 cups of Pecans or other nuts.
1 cup of sugar
1 teaspoon cinnamon
1 teaspoon salt

....

Mix sugar, cinnamon and salt then pour over nut mixture and stir until well covered. Place on cookie sheet and bake at 300* for 25 – 30 minutes. Stir only once then cool and place into covered container.

....

Theo's Pecan Pie

1 stick butter
1 cup dark brown sugar
½ cup dark corn syrup
1 tablespoon vanilla extract
1 tablespoon bourbon
½ teaspoon salt
2 cup whole fresh pecans

....

Cream butter and add remaining ingredients except pecans into unbaked 9 inch pie crust (Homemade or frozen crust) Add 1 cup of pecans to bottom of crust. Pour filling mix over nuts then place remaining nuts on top. Preheat oven to 375 degrees. Bake for 30 minutes then reduce oven to 325 for another 30 minutes or until filling sets (will have a consistency like Jell-O). If crust browns too fast, cover with foil. Remove when done and cool on wire rack.

....

Mother's Buttermilk Pie

1 cup butter or margarine, melted
3 cups sugar
6 eggs
¼ cup flour
1 cup buttermilk
2 tablespoon water
1 teaspoon vanilla extract
½ teaspoon lemon juice
2 unbaked 9 inch pie shells

....

Preheat oven to 350 degrees. Combine butter, sugar, eggs, flour, buttermilk and water in a medium bowl. Stir in vanilla and lemon juice. Mix well. Pour filling into pie shells. Bake for 45 minutes or until firm. Cool pies on wire rack before serving.

....

"He who learns, teaches."
Ancient African Proverb – Ethiopia

Southern Pound Cakes

Special addition: Dedicate our pound cake section to our loving aunties Aunt Katie (Felton) Killins, Aunt Tommie (Felton) Kendricks and Aunt Isabelle (Jones) Beal

"You are not responsible for how people treat you but you are responsible for how you treat other people."

Isabelle Beal (aunt Bit) Cordele, GA

Aunt Kate's Peach Pound Cake

1 cup margarine-softened
3 cups sugar
6 eggs
3 cups flour
¼ teaspoon salt
½ cup sour cream
2 cups chopped fresh peaches
2 teaspoon vanilla

....

Mix margarine and sugar until creamy. Add eggs one at a time beating well after each one then add flour and salt to mixture. Mix sour cream and peaches together in a separate bowl. Fold into flour mixture.

Pour into a lightly grease pound cake pan. Bake at 350* for 75-80 min or until done.

....

German Chocolate Pound Cake

2 cups sugar

1 cup shortening

4 eggs

2 teaspoon vanilla

2 teaspoon of butter flavoring

1 cup buttermilk

3 cups sifted all purpose flour

½ teaspoon baking soda

1 teaspoon salt

1 package German Sweet chocolate

....

Mix sugar and shortening until creamy. Add egg, flavorings and buttermilk. Sift together flour, baking soda and salt; add to creamed mixture. Mix well. Add softened sweet chocolate and blend together well. Bake in 9 in bundt pan that has been greased and floured. or use 2 loaf pans. Bake about 1 ½ hours at 300 degrees. Remove cake from pan while still hot. Place under a tight fitting cake remover and leave covered until cold.

....

Sour Cream Pound Cake

3 cups sugar
3 cups soft butter or margarine
6 egg yolks
¼ teaspoon baking soda
1 cup sour cream (1pint)
3 cusp flour (not cake flour)
½ teaspoon almond extract
1 teaspoon pure vanilla
6 egg whites
Pinch of salt-1 teaspoon

Cream butter and sugar thoroughly. Add Egg yolks one at a time beating after each one. Dissolve baking soda in sour cream. Add alternately with flour. Add flavorings. Fold in the egg whites after beating with salt. Pour into tube pan. Bake in preheated oven at 300 degrees for approximately 1 ½ hours.

Cream Cheese Pound Cake

3 sticks butter
3 cups sugar
Dash of salt
1- 8 oz cream cheese
6 large eggs
1 ½ teaspoon vanilla
3 cups of cake flour

....

Grease and flour 10 inch tube or 12 cup bundt pan. Beat butter and cream cheese until well blended. Add sugar and cream until light and fluffy. Add one egg at a time beating well after each one. Blend in vanilla. Sift together flour and salt. Blend into creamed mixture and spoon batter into prepared pan.

Bake at 325 degrees for 1 ½ hours then Cool in pan 5 minutes then turn unto wire rack to cool completely. Lightly dust with powdered sugar.

....

Buttermilk Pound Cake

1 cup butter
3 cups sugar
5 eggs (at room temperature)
1 cup buttermilk
4 cups flour
1 teaspoon water
2 teaspoon pure vanilla

....

Beat butter until fluffy and gradually add sugar beating constantly while adding one egg at a time. Mix baking soda in water then add to ½ cup of buttermilk. Add 1 cup of flour with milk/soda mixture. Bake 1 ½ hour at 325.

....

Coconut Pound Cake

1 ½ cup butter or margarine
2 ¼ cup sugar
6 eggs
1 teaspoon pure lemon flavoring
2 teaspoon coconut flavoring
3 cups sifted flour
1 teaspoon baking powder
¼ teaspoon salk
1 cup milk
½ cup flaked coconut

Mix sugar and butter until creamy. Add eggs one at a time, beat after each addition. Add flavoring. Combine salt, baking powder and flour. Mix well then add to cream mixture with milk. Fold in coconut. Bake at 325 for 1 ½ hours.

Brown Sugar Pound Cake

1 cup butter or margarine-softened
½ cup shortening
1 box light brown sugar (about 2 ¼ cups packed)
½ cups sugar
5 eggs
2 teaspoon vanilla
3 cups sifted all purpose flour
½ teaspoon baking powder
¼ teaspoon salt
1 cup milk
1 cup chopped pecans

....

Preheat oven to 350 degrees Grease and flour a 10 inch tube pan. Cream butter, shortening and sugars until light and fluffy. Add eggs one at a time beating well after each one. Blend in vanilla. Sift together flour, baking powder and salt then add to cream mixture alternating with milk. Fold in nuts. Spoon batter into prepared pan and Bake 1 hour and 10 minutes or until inserted toothpick comes out clean. Cool in pan for 10 minutes then turn unto wire rack and cool completely and drizzle with Caramel Glaze.

....

Caramel Glaze

½ stick salted butter
½ cup firmly packed brown sugar
¼ cup milk
2 cups sifted powdered sugar
1 teaspoon vanilla

···

Melt butter in small saucepan over medium low heat. Stir in brown sugar, cook 2 minutes stirring constantly. Add milk and continue cooking until mixture boils. Add milk and continue cooking until boils stirring constantly. Remove from heat; gradually stir in confectioners' sugar. Add vanilla; blend well. Drizzle over cooled cake.

···

Chocolate Glaze

2-1 ounce squares of semisweet chocolate
¼ cup butter or margarine
$\frac{1}{3}$ cup sugar
¼ cup milk
2 teaspoon cornstarch
1 teaspoon vanilla

···

Mix chocolate and butter in saucepan over low heat. Stir in sugar, Stir milk into cornstarch and add to chocolate mixture. Cook over medium heat to boil, stirring constantly. Cook and stir 2 minutes longer. Remove from heat. Blend in vanilla. Drizzle over warm cake.

···

Illustrations by:

Lauren Blair